THE CREATIVE WRITING ROCKET

WRITTEN BY LINDA SCHWARTZ: ILLUSTRATED BY BEV ARMSTRONG

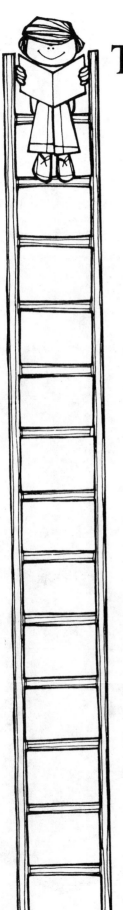

THE LEARNING WORKS

The purchase of this book entitles the
individual teacher to reproduce copies for use
in the classroom.

The reproduction of any part for an entire
school or school system or for commercial
use is strictly prohibited.

THE CREATIVE WRITING ROCKET

CREATIVE WRITING ROCKET CONTENTS

STORY STARTERS

WORD STARTERS

CONTENTS, CONTINUED

PICTURE STARTERS

ABOUT ME

LEARNING CENTER WRITING IDEAS

THE CREATIVE WRITING ROCKET

INTRODUCTION

THE CREATIVE WRITING ROCKET is designed to help motivate even the most reluctant writer in your class. "Catchy" titles and exciting illustrations help stimulate creativity and aid primary students in expressing themselves in writing. Room is provided on each page for the student's work, and stories can be completed on the back or on a separate sheet of paper if necessary.

THE CREATIVE WRITING ROCKET is divided into five sections:

1. STORY STARTERS: Students answer questions on a "fun-filled" topic and then use their answers to complete a story that is already started for them. This section is most helpful for students that have trouble getting started on an idea.

2. WORD STARTERS: Students use a picture plus five words that are spelled for them to develop a story. The words can be underlined as they are used in the story.

3. PICTURE STARTERS: Exciting and creative illustrations are used as the basis for original stories.

4. ABOUT ME: Creative writing based on experiences and feelings of the child—ideal for exploring self-image and values.

5. LEARNING CENTER WRITING IDEAS: A special list of 100 ideas for use at writing centers. Here are several suggested uses for the story titles:

   a. Cut out the titles on narrow strips of paper. Let students draw a slip and write a story using the title.

   b. Let students work with a partner and have each pair write on a chosen topic to share with the class.

   c. Feature one section each week, and let students pick one of the 20 titles from the featured section. Have a STORY OF THE WEEK contest in your classroom.

I SAW A MONSTER

I just saw a monster! (Fill in the blanks.)

1. The monster was as tall as a/an _____.

2. The monster had _____ all over its head and had _____ eyes.

3. The monster was so huge it _____ _____.

4. The monster was so hungry it ate _____ _____.

5. I think I'll call the monster _____.

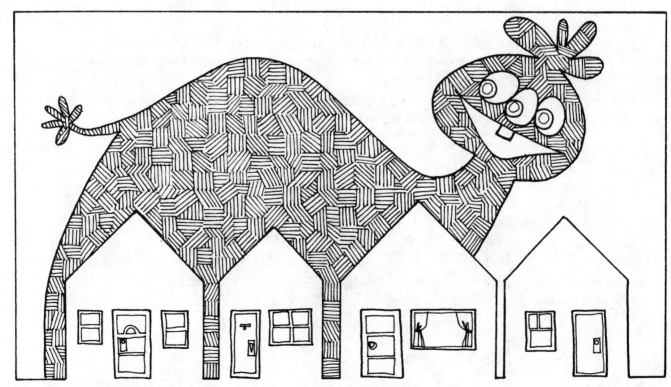

THE CREATIVE WRITING ROCKET

I SAW A MONSTER

Use your answers from the opposite
page. Finish this story that is started
for you.

This is my story about a monster

named_____. I was

the only person who happened to see the monster.

The monster was as tall as_____.

The monster had_____

_____

_____

_____

_____

_____

_____

_____

_____

ME, THE "THING"

You are no longer a person. You are a "thing" such as a book, an airplane, or a toy. (Fill in the blanks.)

1. The "thing" I would most like to

be is a _____.

2. I can usually be found_____

_____.

It's fun to be a penny

GUM

3. The person who owns me is

_____.

4. The best part of being a_____is

_____.

5. The worst part of being a_____is

_____.

I THINK I WOULD LIKE TO BE...

a hammer   a button   a stamp   an apple   a mitten   a ball   a toothbrush

ME, THE "THING"

Being a tennis shoe is hard work!

Use your answers from the opposite page. Finish the story that is started for you.

It is a lot of fun being a

_____.

I am owned by_____.

Most of the time I can be found_____

_____. Here is a story about

something funny that happened to me.

_____

_____

_____

_____

_____

_____

_____

MY SUPER SANDWICH

I made the biggest sandwich in the whole world...
(Fill in the blanks.)

1. My SUPER SANDWICH was as tall as a _____

_____.

2. It was so heavy it weighed_____.

3. This is what I put on my SUPER SANDWICH:_____

_____

_____

4. I had to eat my SUPER SANDWICH with a_____

_____.

5. It took me_____ (hours, days, weeks, months, years)
   (a number)   (circle one)

to finish eating my SUPER SANDWICH.

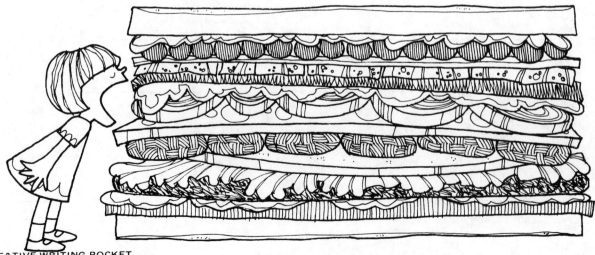

MY SUPER SANDWICH

My SUPER SANDWICH is as tall as a tiger!

Use your answers from the opposite page. Finish the story that is started for you.

I have just made the biggest

sandwich in the whole world!

My SUPER SANDWICH is as tall as a_____

_____. It is so heavy it weighs

_____. You will never believe all

the things I put in my SUPER SANDWICH. I put in

_____

_____

_____

_____

_____

_____

_____

I CAUGHT A KAPEPPER

I just caught a kapepper!   (Fill in the blanks. A

kapepper can be anything you want it to be.)

1. My kapepper looks like a_____and

   a_____ mixed together.

2. I found my kapepper in a_____.

3. The kapepper made a funny noise that sounded

   like_____.

4. I used a_____ to capture my

   kapepper.

5. I will become rich and famous because a kapepper

   is the only thing that can_____

   _____.

My kapepper looks
like a poodle and
a caterpillar mixed
together.

I CAUGHT A KAPEPPER

Use your answers from the opposite page.
Finish this story that is started for you.

It made a funny noise that sounded like a stapler.

CLICKETY - SNAP!

I am the first person in the world

to catch a kapepper! The kapepper

is a mixture of a _____

and a _____.

I found my kapepper in a _____.

It made a funny noise that sounded like_____

_____

_____

_____

_____

_____

_____

_____

THE SHRINK MACHINE

Thanks to the SHRINK MACHINE, you are now about as tall as a pencil. (Fill in the blanks.)

1. I cannot eat hamburgers or hot dogs. I am so small I can only eat_____,

_____, and _____.

2. My bed is too high for me. I will have to sleep in a_____.

3. My bike is too big for me now. I will have to get to school by_____.

4. It is fun being so small because now I can_____

_____

5. My biggest problem being so small is_____

_____.

I will have to get to school by riding on Pickles, my guinea pig!

THE SHRINK MACHINE

Use your answers from the opposite page. Finish this story that is started for you.

I just came out of the SHRINK

MACHINE. I am about the size

of a pencil. I have a big problem eating. I cannot

fit a hamburger or hot dog in my tiny mouth. The

only thing I can eat is _____

_____

_____

_____

_____

_____

_____

_____

A SCARY NIGHT

Look at the picture and the five words.
Write a short story.
Use each of the five words in your story.

ghost
house
rain
lightning
chains

_____

_____

_____

_____

_____

_____

_____

_____

_____

_____

_____

WORD STARTERS
AT THE CIRCUS

Look at the picture and the five words.
Write a short story.
Use each of the five words in your story.

clown   tent   balloon   elephant   popcorn

_____

_____

_____

_____

_____

_____

_____

_____

THE CREATIVE WRITING ROCKET

Copyright © 1976 — THE LEARNING WORKS

THE JUNGLE ADVENTURE

Look at the picture and the five words.
Write a short story.
Use each of the five words in your story.

hunter   jungle   tree   rope   lion

_____

_____

_____

_____

_____

_____

_____

_____

RIDE ON A RAINBOW

Look at the picture and the five words.
Write a short story.
Use each of the five words in your story.

magic   rainbow   gold   cloud   bird

_____

_____

_____

_____

_____

_____

_____

_____

THE GETAWAY

Look at the picture and the five words.
Write a short story.
Use each of the five words in your story.

bank bandits police hero monkey

_____

_____

_____

_____

_____

_____

_____

THE ZOO ESCAPE

Look at the picture and the five words.
Write a short story.
Use each of the five words in your story.

zoo   zookeeper   cage   gorilla   key

_____

_____

_____

_____

_____

_____

_____

_____

THE MAGIC DREAM

Look at the picture and the five words.
Write a short story.
Use each of the five words in your story.

wand   bed   dream   fairy   wish

_____

_____

_____

_____

_____

_____

_____

_____

THE CREATIVE WRITING ROCKET

DANGER BELOW

Look at the picture and the five words.
Write a short story.
Use each of the five words in your story.

boat   shark   diver   ocean   bubbles

_____

_____

_____

_____

_____

_____

_____

THE DOG CONTEST

Look at the picture and the five words.
Write a short story.
Use each of the five words in your story.

dog   contest   judge   ribbon   tail

_____

_____

_____

_____

_____

_____

_____

THE DRAGON'S CAVE

Look at the picture and the five words.
Write a short story.
Use each of the five words in your story.

dragon   fire   boy   girl   cave

_____

_____

_____

_____

_____

_____

_____

ROCKETS AWAY

Write a story about the picture.

_____

_____

_____

_____

_____

_____

_____

_____

THE CREATIVE WRITING ROCKET

A SKUNK IN THE CLASS

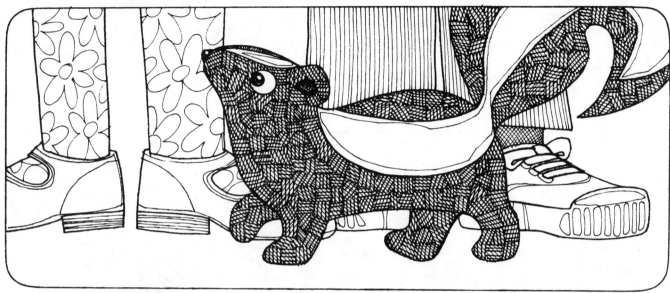

Write a story about the picture.

_____

_____

_____

_____

_____

_____

_____

_____

A VISITOR FROM OUTER SPACE

Write a story about the picture.

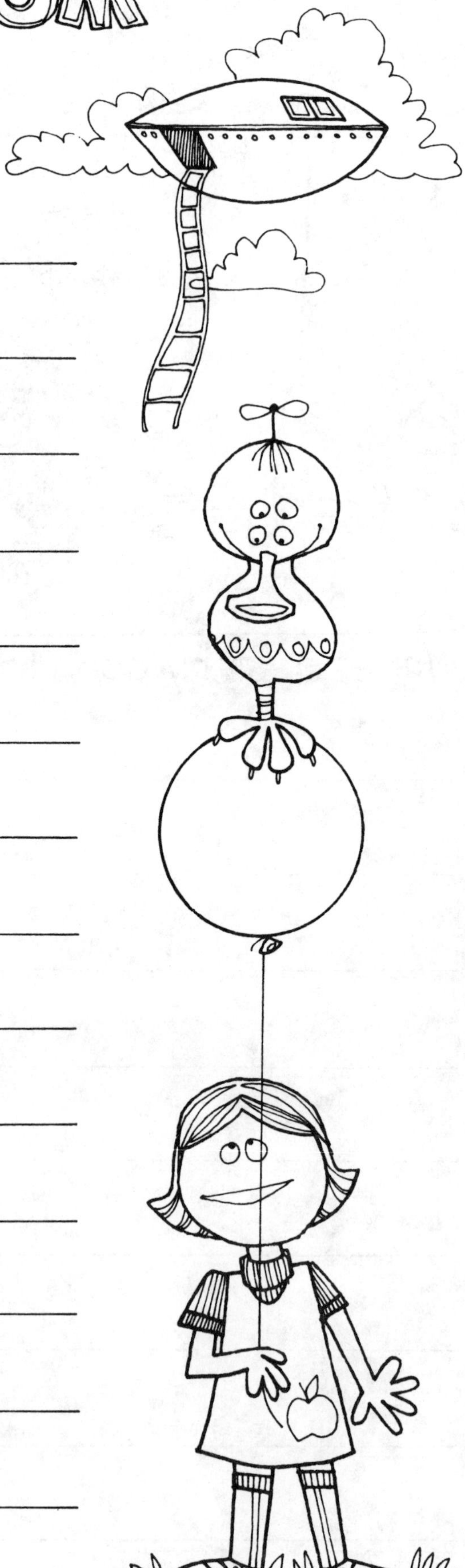

_____

_____

_____

_____

_____

_____

_____

_____

_____

_____

_____

_____

GIVE ME A HOME

Write a story about the picture.

_____

_____

_____

_____

_____

_____

_____

_____

THE DAY IT RAINED CANDY

Write a story about the picture.

_____

_____

_____

_____

_____

_____

_____

_____

_____

_____

_____

_____

_____

THE CREATIVE WRITING ROCKET.

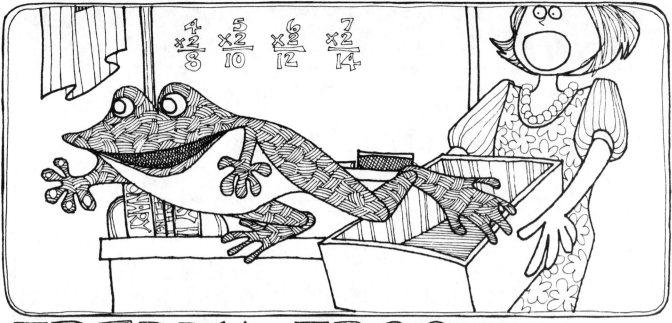

FREDDY FROG

Write a story about the picture.

_____

_____

_____

_____

_____

_____

_____

_____

THE SURPRISE PACKAGE

Write a story about the picture.

_____

_____

_____

_____

_____

_____

_____

_____

_____

IN THE MIDDLE OF THE NIGHT

Write a story about the picture.

_____

_____

_____

_____

_____

_____

_____

_____

_____

THE CRAZY CRITTER

Write a story about the picture.

_____

_____

_____

_____

_____

_____

_____

_____

_____

_____

_____

_____

AWAY ON A KITE

Write a story about the picture.

_____

_____

_____

_____

_____

_____

_____

_____

A POEM ABOUT ME

1. Write the letters of your name going down the paper.

2. Use each letter of your name to begin a line of your poem.

3. Tell about yourself. (What do you like? Dislike?)

Builds tree houses
Red hair and freckles
Is good at kickball
Always telling jokes
Nine is my lucky number

_____

_____

_____

_____

_____

_____

_____

A FUNNY FACT

Here is a story about something funny that happened to me.

_____

_____

_____

_____

_____

_____

_____

_____

THE CREATIVE WRITING ROCKET

THE MAD ME

Here is a story about one time I got very mad.

_____

_____

_____

_____

_____

_____

_____

_____

A SPECIAL PLACE

Here is a story about a very special place I visited.

_____

_____

_____

_____

_____

_____

_____

_____

THE BEST BIRTHDAY

Here is a story about the best birthday I ever had.

_____

_____

_____

_____

_____

_____

_____

THE PERFECT PET

Here is a story about my pet or about a pet I wish I had.

_____

_____

_____

_____

_____

_____

_____

_____

_____

THE WISH MACHINE

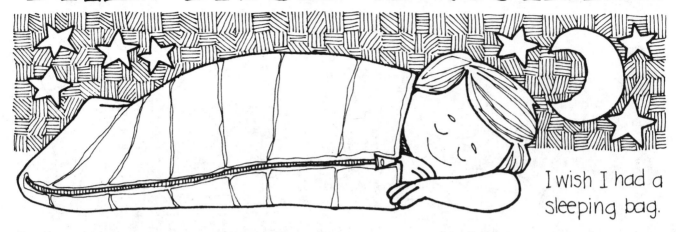

I wish I had a sleeping bag.

Here is a story about a wish of mine.

_____

_____

_____

_____

_____

_____

_____

_____

_____

_____

THE "ING" ME  smiling

Here are three "ing" words that tell about me.

1._____

2._____

3._____

eating

Here are pictures of my three "ing" words.

painting

looking

MONSTERS AND SUCH

1. The Monster on Main Street
2. The Five-Eyed Beast
3. The Haunted House
4. The Creature That Lived in the Lake
5. The Dragon's Cave
6. Caught by a Dinosaur
7. Footprints in the Sand
8. The Tallest Monster in the World
9. How I Captured the "Thing"
10. The Littlest Ghost
11. The Creepy Claw
12. The Monster from Mars
13. The Ghost Strikes Again
14. The Blue Blob That Bubbled
15. The Three-Headed Creature
16. The Monster That Everybody Loved
17. The Tale of the Giant Gorilla
18. The Ugliest Creature Alive
19. The Spider That Grew and Grew
20. The Monster That Took Over the Earth

The Creature That Lived in the Lake

JUST FOR FUN

1. If I Had Four Eyes
2. The Bathtub and the Bubbles
3. The Tree That Grew Candy
4. Miss Mandy and the Popcorn Machine
5. The Surprise Package
6. The Magic Ladder
7. The Bunny Whose Ears Would Not Stop Growing
8. If I Could Ride a Butterfly
9. The Turtle That Could Talk
10. Me and My Flying Boots
11. A Cow on the Roof
12. Dr. Ficklepickle's Secret
13. The Baboon on the Bus
14. The Day I Became Invisible
15. My Life as a Doorknob
16. On the Island of Goochie-Goochie
17. The Story of the Magical Jumping Beans
18. The Clown Who Could Only Walk Backwards
19. The Talking Telephone
20. The Bubble Gum That Would Not Bubble

The Bunny Whose Ears Would Not Stop Growing

ANIMAL STORIES

1. One Puppy Too Many
2. The Bear and the Burglar
3. The Lion that Always Laughed
4. The Snake that Could Bake
5. The Tiger's Toothache
6. A Skunk in My Tub
7. The Pony that Ran Away
8. Dinah, the Dinosaur and the Doughnut
9. A Cat on the Mat
10. Rover Saves the Day
11. The Tallest Giraffe on Earth
12. The Hippo that Could Roller Skate
13. The Big Pet Show
14. The Fish that Could Fly
15. The Littlest Ladybug
16. Sammy Snake and the Teacher
17. Mr. Frog and Mr. Lizard Go to the Movies
18. The Hamster's Hide-out
19. The Squirrel's Silly Joke
20. The Counting Kangaroo

Dinah
the Dinosaur
and the Doughnut

GENERAL STORY IDEAS

1. A Dream Come True
2. A Day I Will Never Forget
3. My Favorite Things
4. The Day We Moved
5. My Big Decision
6. The Surprise Visit
7. New to the School
8. Fun in the Sun
9. A Kid in Trouble
10. Was I Ever Mad!
11. The Best Toy in the World
12. My New Sister (Brother)
13. The Happy Day
14. Fun With My Friend
15. The Big Secret
16. The Day I Got Lost
17. The Best Player on the Team
18. My Hero
19. Just in Time
20. The Chocolate Chip Gang

A DREAM COME TRUE

THE CREATIVE WRITING ROCKET

STORIES WITH A BIT OF COLOR

1. The Boy with the Blue Face
2. The Purple House on Murple Street
3. The Day Green Disappeared
4. The Blue Balloon Escape
5. Lost in the Black Cave
6. The Brown Bear Who Made the Baseball Team
7. The Apple that Grew on the Orange Tree
8. The Day All the Flowers Turned White
9. The Violet that Played the Violin
10. My Life as a Red Raincoat
11. When the Ocean Turned Gold
12. Behind the Gray Door
13. The Orange Pumpkin that Wouldn't Stop Growing
14. The Day It Snowed Silver Snowflakes
15. The Pink Porcupine's Problem
16. The Leopard with Lavender Spots
17. My Ride on a Rainbow
18. Mr. Willy, the Color Wizard
19. The Green Gumdrop Tree
20. The Pink Bubble Gum Machine

The Leopard with Lavender Spots